T0171722

EXPLORE THE PATHLESS JOURNEY TO SELF-DISCOVERY

RISHI AKMAN

BALBOA.PRESS
A DIVISION OF HAY HOUSE

Balboa Press books may be ordered through booksellers or by contacting:

Balboa Press
A Division of Hay House
1663 Liberty Drive
Bloomington, IN 47403
www.balboapress.com
844-682-1282

Bible quotations are taken from the Open Bible, New King James Version, copyright 1997, 1990, 1985, and 1983 by Thomas Nelson Publishers.

Print information available on the last page.

ISBN: 979-8-7652-3563-8 (sc)
ISBN: 979-8-7652-3564-5 (e)

Balboa Press rev. date: 10/12/2022

PRAISE FOR EXPLORE THE PATHLESS JOURNEY TO SELF DISCOVERY

CONTENTS

—————————— ●■● ——————————

INTRODUCTION

Prior to my great awakening, I struggled mentally throughout most of my life, wondering about who I was beyond who I believed myself to be. I had no real sense of purpose or self-worth. Which caused me to desperately seek for my true identity. I start reading every bit of literature that I could find on the mysterious topic of 'who am I'. Passionately, I did not stop there; I purchased self-help audio programs, attended numerous church services, study groups, lectures, and countless seminars. Yet, I found all of my efforts to be in vain. None of which addressed the fundamental question of 'who am I?'. But, after having experienced disappointments after disappointments, I became mentally exhausted in hopes of finding a real answer. So, I decided to stop searching for what seemed to be impossible to fine. Otherwise, I would have continued to cause myself unnecessary mental anguish. It was at this breaking point of suffering; I decided to stop my search and refocus my attention on the ordinary affairs of life. All of a sudden, my then mentor seemingly appeared out of nowhere and introduced me to spiritual attunement through the practice of meditation and self-inquiry. This personal encounter initiated my impersonal pilgrimage into the inroads of self-discovery where the true essence of who I AM exists; a presence that arises from pure consciousness.

I was utterly amazed how simple this process could be, just by turning my mind's attention inwardly upon my inner- awareness through the simple but profound act of self-inquiry. Although the question 'who am I?' remained, I became more optimistic in my quest to explore this unidentifiable aspect of my being— known as Self. As I continued to navigate this pathless journey into the inner-self, I soon realized what I was searching for was always present, and that there was nowhere to go to find it.

Self-discovery is all about awareness, and what you become aware of is without description and cannot be described with words, titles, or labels. This facet of self is the 'I' of your true essence.

Many people strive, mentally, to understand and know the deeper part of themselves in order to establish some meaningful bases for true identity. In this book, Rishi Akman will provide you with the means and methods to initiate your own inquiry into the exploration of the inner self. Much of the book's content reflects an esoteric knowledge expressed in ancient wisdom that is not discussed or practiced among mainstream religions. This knowledge is not of the intellect, but a knowledge that extends beyond your thinking mind, your experiences, your titles, and your labels. Even beyond associations, attachments, and identifications.

These writings are not the thoughts of a single teacher, guru, sage, or any particular group. But a collective consciousness of some of the greatest mystical minds known throughout the ages. Neither is it a religion, belief, or a single philosophy. Instead, it is a written script to direct and guide the unenlightened inquirer into higher conscious awareness of one's inner self.

Unfortunately, until this day, such knowledge is absent within traditional systems of today's religions. However, by reading this book, you will learn some unique applicable techniques that was the central teachings of great masters like Jesus the Christ, the Prophet Muhammad, Buddha, Krishna, and others.

All of which, were examples that reached the state of perfection that corresponded to a definitive fusion between their own consciousness and cosmic consciousness. When humans achieve this fusion, our behavior is then completely in accord with divine laws and fully reflects the greatness, beauty, and wisdom of universal Intelligence. These enlightened beings have attained the highest states of consciousness. Which means they became intuitively aware of their inner essence of self as the true 'I'. They focused their entire being on goodness and used all their will to serve the God within.

A spiritual master gives guidance in a specific and calculated way to still and center the mind to connect with the deeper reality within.

His usual approach is simplified through several practices that can be used to capture this awakening experience, which are the art of yoga, self-enquiry, or by directing your mental focus on the present moment. These methods are very instrumental in accomplishing the goal of self-realization. They play an increasingly important role in your own evolution.

Even without the guidance of such a spiritual master, you can still achieve a desirable outcome as if you were in his very presence.

Although, it is always assuring to have someone who is spiritually equipped to guide you into higher states of consciousness. As well as help you to shorten the learning curve and avoid various pitfalls along the way. We will discuss more in detail about a role of a master in an upcoming chapter.

But if you have not encountered such a person, do not be dismayed. Because these words that are written in this book emanates a distinctive energy that is equivalent to the vibrational frequency of a living master.

And by reading this material, and attuning to its writings and teachings, you give rise to your own energetic 'I' presence. which is the inner master that supersedes any living master that ever existed in physical form.

Take a moment an imagine actually having a living master within you. You become a beacon of light for others to help them explore their own pathless journey into the infinite space of self-discovery.

Such noble achievement can be demonstrated by any sincere person, who ascribe to this light and may not be considered a master but one who is enlighten.

There are several enlighten states to consider; the state of be, being, and becoming. All three states are succinctly integrated but independent at the same time.

- ❖ The state of 'Be' is that state of pure awareness that is unassociated with any personal stories, memories, thoughts, and identifications of being 'this or that'.
- ❖ The state of 'Being' is that state of creativity where the presence of 'I AM' exist.
- ❖ The state of 'Becoming' is that state that unfolds naturally from the unmanifested to the manifested.

All of which, are proactively flowing throughout the human expression as living beings. It is by virtue of these definitions that the evolution of 'self' and its many impressions are understood.

For example: the 'I AM' expression projects itself in the manifested form as being 'this or that' after entering earth realm. Therefore, we become more imperfect in our manifested form due to the descending order of evolution.

Simultaneously, our authentic 'Self' is diminished when integrated with the false notion of becoming 'this or that', which involves the intertwining activity of being and becoming.

Through careful observation, I discovered that most religious people from western societies tend to be more focused on 'becoming'.

They often strive to improve themselves by becoming something more than they perceive themselves to be, which is ego-based rooted in attachments, affiliations, and identifications.

In contrast, many in eastern societies are more spiritually based and tend to be more focused on 'beingness' without a need to become anything else.

However, both societies have their own geographical influences that are shaped, developed and reinforced by their cultural consciousness. Which makes it difficult for each society to focus on both western and eastern approaches equally.

However, in order for both societies to achieve balance. The western society need to slow down and relax into their 'beingness'. While the eastern society need to become more proactive in their 'becoming', rather than just contemplating meditatively, thinking it to be an 'in all-be all' accomplishment.

So, it is important that both societies embrace and focus on both approaches equally. Because, if the state of 'being' becomes purely their focus, which means they are content with themselves exactly as they are with a sense of needing nothing else.

But if 'becoming' becomes purely their focus they will never become awakened or enlightened. Because there will always be distance between 'being and 'becoming' that isolates each society to one approach.

Again, if balance is to occur, the focus of both societies must include 'becoming'— which is a dynamic unfoldment of consciousness that continually manifests in the present state of 'Being'.

Making them perfect in the configuration of their balanced state, while concurrently acting from the substratum underlay of their essence— a state of 'Be'.

Metaphorically speaking, we become as water surfers moving through the crest of waves within the evolving stages of life, which are the states of be, being and becoming.

Unfortunately, this streaming flow of evolution carries us into a seamless series of present moments along with the clinging nature of ego. Figuratively being dragged along the way with its kicking and screaming in the wake of being behind the wave of life, and not ahead of it.

The ego reacts to life after things have happened, rather than engaging with life as things transpires. Its natural compulsive nature is to rule, control and change events that have already happened, in order to declare victory in its false claim of existing. The ego constantly struggles and strives to remain relevant within the evolutional process of Be, Being and Becoming.

That is why it is so important to conduct Self-enquiry, to be able to detect the ego's devious activities. Once exposed, it can no longer maintain its dominating position in the evolutional process.

Start This is the power of Self-inquiry which should not be regarded as a meditation practice that takes place at certain hours with certain postures. Self-inquiry should continue throughout one's waking hours, irrespective of what one is doing. The Truth is that "Self" is a constant presence and can be inwardly observed at all times. The object of enquiry is to find the true nature of the "Self" and to establish its origin. What does it mean to conduct self-inquiry? It means to go beyond the question of who am I? and turn inwardly to investigate the many aspects of self. Self-inquiry is not a mental exercise performed by the mind, but rather an experiential exercise facilitated by the soul— experiencing a sense of self directly and intimately while in higher states of consciousness until a permanent state has been developed. Self-inquiry is a primary point of reference that leads to the soul, which takes us deeper into the spiritual and psychological part of our being. In fact, this psychological construct becomes a doorway into our most fundamental source of Self—the God within.

Self-inquiry is simply the exploration of our inner reality; journeying deeply into the uncharted territory of the psyche and soulish realms of our being without even knowing what is to be expected. Self-inquiry It is not a form of therapy or a self-improvement application, although both can occur simultaneously. When inquiring of "Self", we intuitively probe without having an agenda or a fix plan accept just 'Be"— void of thought, memories, and desires. The only aim in conducting self-inquiry is to discover your truest truth of who you are. Self-inquiry is the first step that leads towards this experience of self-realization, which makes every experience meaningful and not accidental.

Self-realization extends beyond the mental and intellectual mind but often propagated by the inquirer with its inquiry. There is a vibrant presence inside you, wide awake, waiting to be actualized.

All you need to do is turn your attention towards this presence and recognize it as your essential "Self". Which is the essence of your 'Being'— without attributes, forms, distinctions, and external conditionings. This presence is different from what we objectively know, and what we do not know. It is through silence that allows us to access such presence; not by our thoughts nor the use of words that cause us to turn from it without ever finding it.

It has been said by many ancient sages: "The imagination, the understanding, and the abstract thinking will always strive in vain to represent the Infinite". For example, there is no form of finiteness to which thought, and speech can express the Infinite; neither can the timed express the timeless and the eternal. As well as thought resulting from a chain of causation attempting to comprehend the concept of *causeless* or *self-existent*. Any suggestions concerning its qualities, properties, and attributes, the wise simply reply: 'neti, neti'— meaning *'not this'* or *'not that' but* assert that— it is.

The concept of infinite presence is a noble and worthy idea especially when it becomes active within human form, which puts the real 'Self' back in control gradually dissolving the flawed conscious beliefs, emotions and behaviors that have kept us living on autopilot— orchestrated by calculated design through external influences. However, being activity of *doing* does not stop us from "being", because "being" is always present, but doing often lessens our awareness of being in which case it lessens our experience of life. When we are so busy doing, we typically have less awareness of the present moment, which causes us to experience and develop less. But if we can *'do'* and *'be'* at the same time, we gain the best of both worlds. This is what conscious living is all about.

CHAPTER 1

WHO AM I?

—————————————— •■• ——————————————

From childhood to communal and cultural influences we start concealing our inner-Self. We learn social conformity how to adopt and adapt to the ways of the exterior world in order to survive. We are taught by our parents as wells as the educational system what is socially an acceptable behavior. By the time we develop into adulthood, we are completely indoctrinated and conditioned by their beliefs. Which often forces you to function in society according to their goal-oriented-agenda; that is normally conducted by an accepted caste of people who are geared towards materialism and maintaining the status quo. Rarely, are we taught inner development in our early formative years with an emphasis on intuition, higher consciousness, self-awareness, self-esteem, independent thinking, and spiritual evolution. Yet, and despite all the outside influences, the true essence of whom you "are" remains untouched free of any external conditioning.

So, who am I? The world often defines you by your profession, name, nationality, race, or gender. But these descriptions are not who you truly are, even though you may describe yourself in terms of your beliefs, mood, or interests. These are only characteristics that portrays certain personalities that constantly change, so, they cannot be who we truly are. If we look back over our entire life, we will realize that it is only one thing has remained the same throughout our lifetime and that is our true self. Which is the unifying thread that links our early childhood memories to the present moment in an unfiltered way. When we inquire deeper into the felt sense of our awareness of "I-Self", we discover that it has a unique blend of characteristics, qualities, and attributes. It also has an inherent sense of distinctiveness that is far more vital than any personal characteristics that may exist. This must be the essence of who we truly are; in whom there is no shifts, shadows, or variations but a permanent state of the 'I-Self' existence that has experienced every moment of our life.

Unfortunately, we all have forgotten who we truly are in the first few months after birth. However, while we were yet in the womb of our mothers, we had the inception feeling of unity with an inseparable connection. During this stage, our unconditioned and undeveloped mind did not yet have the capacity to conceptualize the idea of self, neither did we know that we were an individual. We were incapable of perceiving and reconciling this new thought of 'being an individual' even with our pre-existing felt sense of true essence and unity. It is not until the age of 9 to 12 months old that our mind would have developed sufficiently enough for us to conceptualize and distinguish 'self' and 'other'. However, we were forced to go with the one and forget about the other in order to avoid conflict between the two. This was mainly due to the conditioning and imposing expectations of others and how everyone else related to us, including our parents, as if we were a separate being; so that is the one we bought into.

As a result, we unknowingly create a false sense of self, known as the ego-self without having anyone to validate our true essence or unity, but only our separateness and physicality. The so called 'other' always interacted with our false-self and pretty much ignored our true-self, so we learned through conditioning to do the same. Essentially, our false 'self' came into being because we were not seen nor addressed for who we truly are, it was only our false self that was constantly being validated, and it became our central identity that had the most and direct influence on our impressionable years to come.

As we grew and developed, so did the false personality of ego along with its many projections making us believe that we are separate from all other existence. This erroneous belief dismisses the concept of oneness and causes us to be under the direct influence of ego. The newly created ego-self was deeply imprinted with an impression of insecurity. So, as our personality developed with the ego-self at its center, our entire personality construct was filled with insecurity. The insecure identity of our ego-self is woven throughout our entire ego personality, so our entire sense of self is insecure, even if we are not consciously aware of this reality. For example, the insecurity of our ego personality becomes very apparent when someone challenges our beliefs, values, or opinions. We immediately become reactive, defensive, aggressive, depressive, or even withdrawn— often setting up egoic-guardrails as a line of defense.

In spite our developed insecurities, emotionally, we quickly learn how to implement coping strategies that enable us to function in life. But there are some personality types try to hide their insecurities behind the falsehoods of exaggerated strengths, false positivity's, and achievements of success; or repress them by seeking justifiable reinforcements to support their mental, emotional, and physical state of being. While others may withdraw to a safe and familiar space seen as their comfort zone, or safe haven, where insecurities cannot be identified or challenged. Let us not forget, there are numerous personality types that reflect certain similar characteristics but are not who we are.

Often our thinking become influenced by the induced traits of the false central core of ego, which creates breeding grounds to provide sponsorship for the ego-self to promote its lies, illusions, and misconceptions. The good news is that our true-Self was never lost, we simply misidentified the ego-self for being our true-Self. In fact, we work extremely hard at maintaining this "I—thought" because we believe it is us and that our life depends upon its continued existence. This existential fear of insecurity underlies many of our thoughts, emotions, and behaviors, which automatically trickles over into other areas of our lives resulting in an identity crisis.

This is why it is so important to turn our attention toward our true Self, be it through self-inquiry or self-analysis. Even though we may have a felt sense of where our true Self exists, does not mean we can simply go directly to it and become Self-realized. There are immeasurable intricate layers of the egoic structure that lay between our innate consciousness— the true Self and conscious awareness. Typically, it becomes a mental hurdle that is difficult to overcome, inhibiting us from realizing our true nature while at the same time generating unaware a false conceptual idea of who we think we are. Suddenly, through misidentification we start oscillating between the ego-self and our body where the ego-self pretending to be our true Self the "I". Not only does the ego pretends to be the real "I", but that the "I" is the body— our felt sense of who we feel we are verses our soul's presence felt sense of being.

The perception and cognitive aspect of our being have become confused with our felt sense of our physical body. This is due to an experiential misidentification associated with body, primarily at our physiological boundary where ends, and the rest of the world of "*This* and *That*" begins; the creative aspect of I AM. In addition, the mass entanglement of the ego structures confuses matters even more by infusing limiting beliefs, reactive emotions, and programmed behaviors. Managing our ego structures is a lifetime venture that can take years before seeing any substantial progress in the area of self-realization due to its complex composition. But when appropriately executed, it is extremely helpful in overcoming the deeper misidentifications of the real Self. Realizing our true Self is often referred to as enlightenment, Self-actualization, Self-awareness, or Self-discovery.

The enlightened phase allows us to dis-identify from the false notions of "I" as being our physical body. However, it is this same "I" that animates our egoic self, otherwise it remains hollow without the vital-life-force that give rise to its existence as well as the body. Subconsciously, we know exactly where to find this "I". But consciously we have no clue and become confused as how to navigate through the puzzling maze of the ego structure. The purpose for inner work is to help you identify, awaken, and release the qualities and energies of the true I. In order to accomplish this, you must become an observer of yourself; carefully watching the settle movement of parading personalities. As the central observer, you become a director on the theatrical stage of your own mental faculties with many actors living inside you. The actors are your different sub-personalities that are responsible for carrying out their assigned roles, which plays a crucial part in your ability to express yourself. The observer (director), role is to assemble, guide, and align these sub-personalities with the inner script of your higher Self for optimal performance to achieve enlightenment. So, take the time to develop the part in you that observes your own process, as no one else can help you do this inner work except for you.

CHAPTER 2

SELF-DISCOVERY

———————————— ●■● ————————————

Self- discovery, in the true sense of the word, is a pathless passage into the journeying of your essential nature. This is an inward voyage that is travelled by a relative few and must be taken alone. But for those who manage to pivot their consciousness toward the awareness of Self, will achieve their highest potential to bring about a transformation on all four planes of existence— physically, mentally, emotionally, and spiritually. Spontaneously giving rise to a deeper sense of self and the emerges of as the projection of 'I AM', which lay dormant in most people until it is awaken through the act of self-inquiry. In this discovery of Self, one realizes that the 'I am' is the awareness that exist and is witnessed by the existing "I" itself. This is the mysterious inner workings and enfoldment of your own infinite divine nature that imbues the collective consciousness within life.

Self-discovery is not achieved by adhering to any particular systems of belief, but by understanding the process of spiritual evolution and how to appropriately apply spiritual principles that are in harmony with and governed by universal laws— the mind of God. I will not attempt to define the nature of this infinite deity, but rather leave it to your own discovery. Nonetheless, the very essence of this involution goes beyond the five physical senses, which gives rise to insightful creativity and innovative solutions to attune to these governing laws within the universe.

This is the gateway into the infinite source of insight that let you see yourself in an impersonal way; affording you the blissful opportunity to ascend to higher consciousness to experience direct union with God. While at the same time making you consciously aware of your true self— "I am", without associating it as being the physical body. So, how does one identify himself as a living being within the context of 'I' or 'I am'? does he view himself as the Thinker— apart from his thought? the Doer—apart from his action? or the Feeler— apart from his feelings. The universe is a direct reflection of our God-Self that is expressed through your free-will— the primary function of self. you are not required to accept anything by faith or belief, but simply think for yourself and conduct your own self-inquiry to draw upon the higher knowledge that already exist within you.

Once there has been an awakening to this level of consciousness, the false sense of self veiled in the shadow of illusions and forms soon dissolves. However, in higher consciousness, your true remains intact and interconnected with life existence. Although the intellectual mind perceives all distinctive forms and appearances as being real— seemingly to be separate from yourself. But, when you understand how the intellectual mind works with the influence of ego, you will no longer view yourself as being an object separate from others but being one in consciousness with all. There are two aspects of separateness to consider— the subjective and objective. Both can be quite confusing for the untrained and undeveloped mind, which makes it difficult to discern the difference between something 'within' and 'something without'— the subjective and objective. In absolute reality, no person can be the object of his own thoughts, feelings, or ideas.

Objectively speaking, man cannot know the essence of himself but only his outer appearance. However, in the gradual enfoldment of the subconscious mind, there is a higher existence of self-consciousness that is always aware of its existence and realizes that it is the individual "I". Instead of being merely a bunch of subjective thoughts, feelings, emotions, and desires or an objective appearance of the body. But we must not fall into the error of assuming that a man or even the less-developed individuals possess this faculty of awareness to any high degree. However, during this stage of his mental evolution the essence of self is discovered, and it knows that I AM I; the first born of the cosmic consciousness.

Even after achieving such development, he may experience a feeling of fear when he first come to realize the true or 'Self'. Because there is a sense of loneliness that arises making one feel detached from all other things; be it people, places, or things, which is considered to be normal. But in the face of, all self-claimed identifications will fall away, and the feeling of separateness and apartness grows less acute as the consciousness of I-ness increases. Yet, this aspect of the personality— egoic I, will always be present to a greater or lesser degree until a higher level of conscious awareness is attain. One must remain watchful and aware of this morbid state employed by the egoic when coming into this sense of. It has the tendency to present itself has the real; or "Self" to avoid detection and prevent the process of the individual's transformation.

The ego will further attempt to obscure your ability to discern its whereabouts by hiding itself among the other sub- personalities of its own creation; to avoid being eradicated in order to maintain its current position for future control. Perceivably, the introspection phase of "Self" can seem to be quite painful; having to let go of familiar attachments, old beliefs, and false identities that reinforces the erroneous thoughts and ideas as to who and what you really are. unfortunately, many entangled themselves in the conundrum of this mental state not knowing that this process can become more painful as the individual advances in his awareness of self-consciousness, and as he nears the end at which he is to find deliverance. This reminds of the biblical story of Adam when he decides to eat and share the forbidden fruit from the tree of knowledge with his wife Eve. Suddenly, both begins to suffer and is driven out of the Garden of Eden, which is symbolic of a falling state from Self-consciousness— the 'I am'. In this state, he does not concern himself with the affairs of his higher nature, but rather continue to chase his desires prompt by the human appetite; therefore, he continues to suffer.

The more he desires; the more does he suffer from the false perceived pain of not having. He has not only the pain of unsatisfied cravings and unfulfilled desires for possession of material things, as well as physical needs, but his inability to provide intelligent solutions to the ever-increasing struggle induced by the untrained mind. After having spent valuable time wallowing in his own fabricated misery, he then searches outwardly for methods, means and ways to escape his current condition. He labors ceaselessly to connect with others who may have had similar experiences in hopes of finding a solution for himself. Even if it is only for some mental stimulations induced through conversation to make him feel better about himself. No matter the subject, concept, or idea that is being discussed, in most cases, all of which appeals to the Intellect and promotes logical thinking only, which is known to be head knowledge that limits his ability to experience direct knowing.

As a consequence, he continues harnessing his Intellect to the chariot of unbridled desires and drive it along by command of his self-serving will; causing the chariot driver—ego to become disappointed, frustrated and disorientated drifting astray further into the delusional false sense of "self. As man continue to move in his destructive unrestrained passions for new wants becomes more and more complex, because he mentally attaches himself to "things," and create for himself artificial wants which he must work hard to acquire and maintain. His intellect fails to lead the lower aspect of his being upward toward his higher consciousness where he can invent new ideas and concepts that are totally satisfying. Instead, he becomes vain, conceited, and filled with an inflated egotistical personality with a false sense of self-importance. In this state, he cannot properly analyze, control, or manage his sensations, moods, drives, or impulses as does a drunken man. He becomes mentally impaired and lessens his capacity for true lasting pleasure by succumbing to the appetite of the lower vibrations of his passions.

These external bates are designed to keep him looking outside of himself rather than within. But once he reaches this state of higher consciousness, the shadowing personalities of ego is exposed by its vivid light. Giving him a clear mental pathway to return to his original state of 'I Am', where he is delivered from his entire burden of mundane appetites that makes his suffering, restoration, transitioning and ascension worthwhile. Afterwards, he is awakened to new levels of awareness gradually detaching his sense of 'Self' from its false casing of ego to the realization of 'I Am'. At this point, it become clear to him that all thoughts, ideas, feelings, emotions, and desires, are but visitors; they come and go with no permanency in their visitation. So, they are to be viewed as drifting clouds, simply passing by, that will soon give away to clear skies that is without change. But, comparatively so, he perceives himself to be "I Am" surrounded by his five senses—as the Sun is surrounded by its revolving worlds and terrestrial activities.

Subsequently, he soon realizes that the ego acts superior to his mind, body, and feelings by it taking control and dictating to his thoughts, actions, and emotions. So, the mind becomes the ego's main target because every thought or action first occur within the mind and without the mind there can be no mental or physical activity at all. The ego needs to feel alive and be in control to further validate it existence so that the mental construct remains captive to it unbridle impulses and strongholds. If he is to take back control of his mental faculties, it is imperative that he began exercising mastery over his own thoughts and feelings to break free the rulership of ego. Self-mastery empowers one to control all mental thoughts, as well as, put in check the cunning tactics of the ego; a personality whose presence is always there, on the prowl, seeking to fulfill its every desire.

Once these yearnings of the ego are neutralized, he will no longer be ruled by its influence, but instead employ dominion over them. He essentially rules from a higher state of consciousness that frees himself from mental torment and gives him reigning authority and command over his total being. Allowing him to psychologically expand into the awareness of his true 'Self'; a state of consciousness that was once unbeknownst to himself. Where he is able to develop the ability to withstand the ego's sphere of influence and continue to subdue the adversarial forces of the egoic nature within. Not only does he become a master of mind, but a ruler in every aspect of his psychosomatic being. Permitting the real with its selfless attributes and qualities to become superior to his entire mental construct to include his five senses. Which empowers him to influence other parts of his mental faculties and align with the consciousness of, which is Self and the master of thoughts, feelings, and desires. For this is the internally discovery, reality, and power of the "I".

Such governance by the requires a certain type of unwavering attention, although it is limited in its reservoir of capacity and output. The attention span of an average human being is about 8 seconds—ten minutes at max, which is considered to be exceptional; even at the highest level of intellectual processing. To exceed this span of time, requires a measurable amount of mental training that involves deep concentration as well as a laser beam focus. Or the guidance of someone who knows and has demonstrated the acumen and competence in this area. Attention is an inherent apparatus that plays a significant role in self-realization, and for those who wish to go beyond sheer speculation of 'Self' must give their exclusive focused attention to the awareness of self. It is important to draw wisely from the limited resources of 'attention' to make ready and good use of it when given or directed.

CHAPTER 3

THE UNDEVELOPED HYBRID MAN

———————————— • ■ • ————————————

Man, in his current state has a keen desire to know himself and the significance of his position here on earth. But has no known method to realize and address his desire that emerges forcibly and burns deeply within himself. His best initial approach is to start with things based on the elements that exist in his own environment, which only leads him further away from what is real into the illusion of who he thinks himself to be. Therefore, he continues seeking for knowledge in things outside of himself that only serves to reinforce the egos false sense of knowing. This type of knowing is restricted to the head only; a mental accumulation of stored data that can never provide him with the understanding and true meaning of himself as well as his life's mission.

Consequently, preventing the seeker access to direct knowing of himself— known as Gnosis. But once he has reached a certain stage in his own evolution of knowing, he immediately gives rise to true knowing that moves it from the head to the heart-center where the true knowing exist. He then realizes the mental knowledge acquired is illusionary in nature and his truth of being is not to be discovered outside himself but within. Essentially, he becomes the object of his own study being both the lab and lab-technician. However, it is through this self-study — Gnosis, he establishes and validate his intuitive findings regarding the true knowledge and nature of "Self". In addition, he becomes an I-witness to his own introspective discovery.

Every person possesses their own individual laboratory but fail to be the lab-tech of their own investigational inquiry. This is a mis-opportunity for the inquirer to get an in depth understanding of his me-construct and its function that can possibly authenticate his inner experience. Therefore, he continues to live life in a mechanized way, never developing the power of concentration nor the time required to pause from the detractions of life to investigate himself. He spends his days completely absorbed by his worldly affairs without any inner observation at all. Ceaselessly engaged in day-to-day rat-race of mechanical activities until he exhausts himself; never accomplishing anything worthwhile. Seemingly, life passes by almost unnoticeably as like a 'blink of an eye' causing him to remain a stranger to himself.

He is constantly consumed and pressured by the demands of life leaving no time to investigate the individual or 'Self', causing him to drift deeper into the matrix of illusions where there is perpetual change with no continuity. If by some chance he decides to pivot inwardly, and to his surprise, he will realize and locate the thing he was once desperately searching for. I would be remiss if I fail to remind you that there is multiple 'I's that exist in one man, all of which are incredibly bundled and bound up together; the individual 'I', the egoic 'I', and the personality 'I' not to mention the many sub-personalities. Comparatively so, the Individual 'I' is the only constant station among them all; holding a status of permanency and not a temporary state of beingness as does the other existing "I's. The false 'I' of the personality and its many sub-personalities are always competing for a position to dominate and rule the me-construct, each having its own cravings, preferences, and undertakings. These autonomous impressions come more into focus while inter-face with his inner awareness, which gives him the ability to continue his inner exploration and experimentation with less distractions from the other perpetrating 'I's.

However, among the awaken ones; there exists a great appreciation and value for introspection as a practical means to self-discovery, enabling the practitioner to understand and examine himself thoroughly. His internal makeup is similar to that of a vase filled with filings of iron shavings that are often fused by mechanical action. For example, the fragmented filings become displaced and takes on new shapes and formations at every external blow to the vase. This is likened to mans' mental state, he becomes consciously oblivious to the relative activities of life due to constant change occurring in his inner state of being, which is generally caused by external circumstances.

For every encounter there is a mental shift in thoughts that produces more fragmented thoughts. Similar to the activities that takes place within the vase, he becomes mentally unstable in the most unnoticeable ways. However, it is through the power of Introspection that he can produce an intense friction among these internal shavings of thoughts to create an inner fire that kindles within him to burn away other unneeded filings. This process works to his advantage, bringing about a fusion among the shavings of inner thought and to congeal his various personalities to avoid future displacement. In Essence, allowing him to keep his psychological and mental faculties intact. But this requires hard work by making a conscious effort to carefully keep the fire burning once ignited. He literal becomes the watchman of his own soul.

Henceforth, man's inner content will no longer be a conglomerate of shavings exemplified by fragmented thoughts, but a mental construct forged as being whole as one unit. Having reached this point of transformation, he will have acquired enough mental strength to undergo any storm of life and not be shaken by outside circumstances. But before he can achieve this state of consciousness, he must first eliminate any illusions that he has about himself no matter how appealing they may appear to be. Refusal to do so, will cause the illusion to increasingly grow creating more false impressions. Which interns cause more mental anguish an unnecessary suffering preventing him to escape such illusion. If he failed to achieve the fusion stage, he will continue living an artificial life unaware of his inner change, which are triggered by the external blows he receives from outside of himself.

He lives at the mercy of life unfolding events as a tattered victim, preoccupied by constantly patching-up shattered pieces and being led by chance in the direction of the chaos. However, the practice of introspection clearly show that everything is changing within us every moment— timeless and unmeasured. Yet, man ignorantly claims to have some continuity in his thoughts, speech, and actions; he gives his word, makes promises, and takes vows that bind him despite these perpetual changes that he has notice in himself. Which makes him double minded in all of his ways and incapable to make good of his word.

This is a true indication and root cause for his ever-reoccurring problems in life to include his inner and external conflicts, which makes up the greater portion of his life experiences. Nothing is stable about him; he is quick to defend his unstable behavior by attempting to justify his action through the influence of the egoic 'I'. The ego cunningly and convincedly makes him believe that he is the master of his own actions, and that he is clearly aware of all and any changes that occurs within him. And that all of his activities were foreseen and pre-calculated in advance. This is him pretending to be in control. But when things get out of hand and becomes unmanageable for him, abruptly he cast the blame on others, his circumstances, or some external event.

This is because the friction of the mental shavings of thought produced a disagreeable impression that caused unstable shifting within his mental faculties. The movement and shifting of these fragmented shavings of thought cease to be when a solution is found, subsequently neutralizing the jolts received by surrounding forces and external conditions.

To find what or whom to blame— is to find the essential solution for transformational change. As previously mentioned, man is continually preoccupied with this inner patching-up as a quick fix for resolving his state of disarray. This being the case, how then can these internal changes be characterized? What and who is changing? When man refers to himself, He speaks in the first person 'I' and It is perhaps the most mysterious term unconsciously used in the human language. But an awaken person realizes the I'ness of his beingness is neither the body nor soul, although it may seem puzzling to the unenlightened man. So then, you may ask what is man if he is neither body nor Soul? What is his self-claimed "I"? which he believes to be himself.

Comparatively so, it is precisely the particles of the non-fused and unstable composition of the shavings of thoughts that constantly changes, which represent the egoic 'I' in us. This 'I' is not stable, it has many different aspects but is nevertheless the 'I' with which man's personality is shaped, conditioned, and developed. Also, the egoic 'I' is the host of multiple coexisting sub-personalities along with their interchangeable traits which are not a permanent fixture within the assembly of the egoic 'I'. Because they come and go without trace or notice. In fact, these small I's are relatively independent with each behaving differently in their own way reflecting the nature of the egoic 'I'.

The question remains, who is man? Still, in his limited understanding of himself, he can only conclude that there are other entities that lives within him that constantly change with every impression they receive. You may be thinking to yourself: who can escape such dilemma? Only someone who can control his thoughts and master his impulsive and instinctive responses that generates mechanical displacement of the sub-personalities. For what is prevailing within man is the law to preserve the internal micro bits of shavings from anarchical aftereffects. This is only possible after having pivoted toward the real 'I' and truly become master of himself causing him to be unshakable with unmeasurable interior calm even after receiving a displacive blow of exterior circumstances. It is imperative that man becomes master of himself in order to attain such higher state of consciousness that causes him to rise beyond the false fabricated I's.

To know and master thyself requires an act of Introspection, self-inquiry, and a sincere study into the function and structure of one's personality. Knowledge is power, applied knowledge is empowering but self-knowledge is liberation. As he continues his inner probe, he will soon discover that there is a three-dimensional aspect to 'self' that streams from his psychic, intellect, and instinctive mechanism that performs in concert without any clear-cut line of division. All of which, have a direct correlation to his thoughts, feelings, senses. The center gravity of each aspect of his psychic assembly rest perceivably in the brain, heart, and loins. when an impulse is received or sent out from any one of these three centers, the two others adopt a passive posture as active participants while giving way to the one. Which is momentarily in command performing in part as the whole of his personalities, which inadequately represents the total man.

These three centers have a dual function within the various aspects of his personalities— receptive and expressive. The mental structure and its modalities are magnificently formulated, since each center in its respective field is perfectly suited for the needs of man's inner and outer existence. The human personality is an active aspect of his beingness that serve as a channel for psychic organism to express its existence. The personality is always at play, even without being aware of it, or without having a clear understanding of its nature and subtle movements. therefore, it is important for the inquirer to study the structure, content, and inner workings of his personality in order to understand the psychological functions of the three centers:

1)   The psychic center: are presumptively the center of gravity and it directs instinctive components as well as mechanical forces of psychological activities that are disseminated throughout the body.

2)   The intellectual center: registers, thinks, calculates, contrives, seeks out, the emotional center; the feelings, as well as the reinforced sensations and delicate passions.

3) The mechanical center directs the five senses, accumulates energy within the organism through its instinctive functions and manages through its motive functions with the utilization of this source of energy.

The mechanical center is the best organized of the three. On the other hand, the first two centers can be problematic. They are anarchic in nature and frequently intrude on each other's territory, to include the motorized center. In fact, we have neither pure thoughts, pure feelings, nor pure actions due to the mixture of all three centers, each propagating its own calculations within our physiology make-up.

Therefore, it is imperative to call order to our psychic construct and dismantle the state of perpetual anarchy so that we can subjectively study the structure of our personality in detail. This study enables the inquirer to understand the mechanical functioning of this internal organism that brings about perfect harmony amongst the three centers. But the only way to achieve this outcome is to work on oneself through the act of introspection. This type of self-examination is apparently the most difficult for most people do, mainly because of their mental conditioning, which leads them to complicate any future efforts.

In addition, when it comes to studying the personality and its inner workings there must be a certain type of knowing and understanding present. However, in correlation to both knowing and understanding are indicative of one another; knowing can exist without understanding, but understanding cannot exist without knowing. So, understanding is knowing with something unquantifiable added to it. Ironically, the description is simple yet complicated. The transference from knowing to understanding is in direct proportion to the integration of realization. The function and capacity of absorption is limited, which varies in every person.

For instance, if you were to pour the content of a pitcher into a glass it would suddenly cause an overflow spilling forth its substance.

Which means the volume of liquid within the pitcher is not equivalent to the capacity of the glass. In similar ways, this is exactly what transpires within in human beings. As an equivalent, we are only capable of understanding what corresponds to the capacity of our intellectual construct. For example, when Jesus the Christ spoke to his disciples saying, "I have yet many things to say unto you but ye cannot bear them now" (John 16:12 KJV).

He was basically telling them they must first expand and raise their level of awareness in consciousness, in order to understand the true and implied meaning of his words. Which were spoken from a place of intuitive insight that are worth being reflected upon. His use of language was designed to point them in the direction higher consciousness where there are four levels to be considered:

- ❖ Firstly, the sub-consciousness— that is the twilight consciousness of the body; Its strength is independent of the cultural level of the individual, which occur during sleep and is responsible for the functioning of our involuntary system to include the awaken state.
- ❖ Secondly, the waking consciousness— the aware consciousness of the personality that expresses the cultural development of the individual; It is the subjective consciousness of the 'I'.
- ❖ Thirdly, the consciousness of the real 'I'— the consciousness of the Individuality of self or the objective consciousness of the individual 'I'.
- ❖ Fourthly, the real 'I'— an inert state of consciousness that realize itself to be the only permanent component station within us that is independent of all other fabricated I's within the egoic personality.

The ego is constantly changing its identity among the sub-personalities with the reinforcement of endless stream of thoughts, feelings, passions, and sensations causing man to act impulsively. On the other hand, the consciousness of the real 'I' is always just and objective. The real I only expressions itself in a passive form; until the egoic personality acquiesces its acts to the real I's ruling. In everyday life, the contact with our real 'I' occur extraordinarily— it is always present. Yet, man proclaim to function from a corresponding place of his real 'I'. That exemplifies a false sense of its qualities, and attributes pretending to be logically stable with having the willpower and ability to perform on a higher level of consciousness.

Such a false notion has a destabilizing consequence, further masking the present consciousness of the true 'I'. However, an objective examination of this apparent fact proves sufficient to validate this proclamation. Simply because we are not functioning from the essence of the real 'I' but from the level of the waking-consciousness— the egoic 'I' of the personality. Most of the times we identify with whatever the impression it presents carrying us further into the masquerading of the small I's within the egoic personality. Each wanting to fulfill its own desire while acting out with erratic behaviors consistently swinging back and forth between decision and results clinging to that which seems to be most pleasurable.

Because of their unpredictable nature, they will shift in a moment's notice by giving way to other small I's, which may disapprove of both the decision and results. Sometimes these sub-personalities become so radical in their instincts until it seems as if a stranger had acted on his behalf. Often times the true self is eliminated from the decision-making process, which brings consequential regrets later. Which is due to the dualistic nature of his being; explicitly the qualities belonging to his egoic 'I'.

However, it is possible for man to achieve this level of consciousness, when awakening to his real 'I', even though a considerable amount of mental work is required, it must be coupled with intense effort and determination made by the inquirer, before what he claims to attain becomes evident. So long as man continues to be satisfied with himself as he is in his current condition. He will continue living in a world of irrationality and irrelevance mistaking his desires and his self-fabricated illusions for absolute reality. In order for him to evolve to a higher plane of consciousness, he must undergo bankruptcy within his egoic system causing an inner structural collapsing and meltdown of its sub- personalities. There must be a total dismantling of the 'me construct' without attempting to reassemble the fragmented pieces of the false I's that he claims to be himself. It is only then, that he can begin to look inwardly with clarity to obtain the necessary insight to work on every level of his being. This is true for every person who desires to be transformed.

The I's of the sub-personalities makes a man believes himself to be someone of considerable importance. In fact, we all fall victim to this illusionary self to some degree even for those who claim to be awaken. This false notion of importance of these sub-personalities that are the sum of our human qualities and faults, which are the same for every person despite cultural, social, and economic differences. However, the I's of the sub-personalities it is a measure of the whole as being an integrated component of man's sum total that equates to zero – a state of wholeness, which can be interpreted by those who are high minded as being nothing.

Nonetheless, this is starting place for him to free himself from the illusional afflictions that he has created, while at the same time restoring his fragmented personality to a state of wholeness. I cannot put it in better words than what was proclaimed by the Christ Jesus, "They that are whole have no need of the physician, but only they that are sick" (Mark 2:17). Figuratively so, this speaks to the idea of salvation; mending the fragment pieces of his multi-personality to create unity within the whole of man's being— the mind, body, and soul. This is the salvation work of transmutation likened unto being born again—the salvaging of man.

As he matures and transition from his newborn state, he then forms new concepts within himself that are directly in alignment with the higher consciousness of his true 'I'. Causing him to arise from his immersed state of personhood into a permanent station of the impersonal 'I'. Therefore, he is now considered to be the perfect man in his ongoing development, even though noticeable flaws may still exist. However, the real 'I' remains perfect and unflawed. He is no longer mentally influenced by the unstable 'I' of his ego, nor by its sub-personalities that can disrupt the harmonious progression between his actions and ideas.

His actions are generated through intellectual knowing and his ideas through intuitive knowing. Both are intrinsic in nature fostering a dual activity— a passive form and active form. Intellectual knowing is an active form that is formulated by collective memories and past experiences. whereas Intuitive knowing is direct knowing (Gnosis); a passive form that is formulated by pure consciousness.

However, both knowing's are governed and directed by infinite wisdom to ensure appropriate application. It is relatively easy to acquire intellectual knowing, but to develop Intuitive knowing is more difficult to accomplish due to external conditioning. Intuitive knowing provides us with both the understanding and knowhow even during the interplay of multiple I's. Each bearing its own name as for the basis of its existence and appearance. The personal 'I' and sub-members reinforces their validity through past experiences that are fixed in memory. By assign individual names to each 'I' that corresponds to the 'I' of the active personality irrespective of the relative position and action that it may formulate.

The corresponding 'I' of the personality, with its selected name, reflects the image that man has of himself in his waking state of consciousness, which can be defined by him as being real. Identification is a direct link to memory and memory is a precise function of the brain that plays a role in the formation and mental storage of man's cognitive state. The higher level of cognition; the stronger the memory is with a greater capacity of retention. Loss of memory leads to the loss of identification along with the name that is attached to it, which makes a man to feel insignificant and without purpose. This is also true for the individual whose identity have been stripped away.

While In this condition, he ceases to inquire about his identity, instead subsists in his true essence of absolute consciousness— a symbolic place of zero meaning nothing. In this space of nothingness, he eventually realizes this is the space of his true Self; free of any conceptual identities or formulated attachments; such discovery is the crowning achievement known to humankind. The path to the true self is a pathless journey without measurable distance and with no trace to follow except for the inner-witness of man's awareness— the unmanifested individual 'I'. This unmanifested 'I' imbues an evolutional impulse within man inner being that causes him to evolve from a phenomenal state of 'be' into the enfoldment of 'becoming'. Further descending through the corridors of time and space, spiraling into the formation of life manifesting in human form expressing its noblest virtue of 'being'.

But still, the fundamental questions remain for many, who am I? What is my true nature? What is the meaning and purpose of my existence? Out of pure curiosity, any inquiring person would ask these self-probing questions not realizing that self-inquiry is the first step toward an inward search to discover one's true self? In our best attempt, can we truly answer the most essential of all questions, specifically, who am I? or more so, what am I? and why was I born? These inquires will always remain a mystery to a seeker until he gives less focus to his personal identities and worldly involvements, with its addictive activities, and turn his full undivided attention to the awareness of self.

Any other approach will leave a sincere seeker unsatisfied with not having to acquire the needed answers, but rather bring him back to the original questions— who am I, what am I? and why was I born? Intellectual answers will not provide a solution for such identity crises. Unfortunately, there is no way to escape this line of questioning except through the awakening to Self— the true essence and testament to who and what you are as well as why you exist. Until one comes into this place of awareness in sincerity, it is important to continue pondering and peering into the question who am I? Which causes him to direct his thinking and focus his attention inwardly towards the origin of his existence and not towards external objects.

As a result, He enters a state of not-knowing. This state has no path, directional indicators, symbols, or labels to reference and base his findings upon. Leaving him to live with the profound-ever-perpetuating questions of the three W's. However, by living with the questions does not mean he has to seek a conclusion or answer. Because the question, in and of itself, is the answer. Its identity is unidentifiable originating from the eternal parent that gives birth to the I and the various states of I AM— be, becoming and being as his evolving Self.

We all possess this evolving centerfold of self; for it is a fundamental principle that gives full expression within our beingness. Nobody can tell you who you are because It would be just another false identification assigned to self, which does not render a true answer or description of your essence. Such realization requires no belief, in fact, belief at its best is flawed and shifty in nature without continuity. Neither does the essence of who you are requires your realization, in order for it to exist, because the essence of who you have always existed before you became aware of it.

The moment you realize this reality of 'who you are', you immediately connect with the true nature of your existence, which is an unmanifested state that is free of false identifications. Sadly, most people are unaware of their own inherent nature. It is likened to a poor man who does not know he has an inheritance of wealth available to him, so his existing resources remains untapped as does your essential self; an unexpressed potential that arises from a space of the unknowable that leads one to say, "I don't know". It is in this reply of "I don't know" that there is something knowable— an oxymoron of dualism.

Even at this level of understanding, still, more significant questions may arise such as, what is this existing I? Where does this 'I' come from? and when or does it die, and if so, where does it go? These are the most basic questions you can ever ask. This 'I' is the essence of who you really are, which consist of all things— it is the unmeasurable innate substance that springs forth from pure consciousness. This substance is embedded in all of creation, and even in the elements of nature that bares its imprint. Such as the sun, moon, stars, mountains, rivers, and trees to include celestial beings. All of which are of the same substance that are supported and animated by the substratum forces of life that never dies, which is the essence of your true self— the station of I.

CHAPTER 4

THE APPROACH TO SELF-INQUIRY

— ●■● —

Self-inquiry is the key to potentially awakening to your deep sense of awareness that reveals all that is true within you whereas neither the ego, mind, or intellect can. After having realized the true self, nothing else remains to be known except for the pure and unconditioned self. Such insight enables one to realize that self-inquiry is the one and only direct approach to this source of knowing— it is the first born of pure consciousness. A space of awareness that is unstained by conceptuality, which implies that there is a total absence of beingness— a nonexistent object; where there can be no 'it' to bear a name, because no assigned name is possible where no object exists.

Furthermore, pure consciousness is a timeless and spaceless substance of energy that is forever present designed to awakening the soul from its slumber state. But to employ any other effort to awaken oneself apart from consciousness itself will be fruitless; it would be like trying to gain access into the spiritual world through the act of religious rituals. Let's be clear, religious activities has it place in the greater scheme of things. Because such activities can be used to inspire one to mentally position himself to receive a greater dawning of understanding as to the active force emanating from pure consciousness; where the existence of the real 'I' emerges and take full expression within his being that makes for his actual reality.

But when this source of consciousness is ignored or forgotten, one falls victim to the governance of the false 'I' of ego, which is generally the triggers mental suffering generated by the instinctive nature of desire. However, when one is fully aware of his true 'I' in consciousness he can resist the control of ego by practicing mindfulness. which can be conducted or practiced anywhere at any time... preferably in a quiet place free of distractions. But be aware of imposing questions that may enter your mind while engaged in your quiet space, such as how to realize the Self— I? or can the self be found? If so, where? Nonetheless, do not be distracted by these arising questions, but allow them to occur without giving significant meaning to them.

However, it is important to ask yourself who is inquiring? and who is observing the one inquiring? Then you may say to yourself "I do not know?" I say, find that somebody within, who is doing the inquiring and who is doing the observing, then you can trace its source. The secret is to mentally hold to the single thought of who am I? which will prevent other unwanted thoughts to emerge; it is impossible to focus on two thoughts at one time. Once Again, when other thoughts arise, do not identify with them but simply observe and inquire with diligence by asking yourself from where did these thoughts arise? Normally, the answer will be from me. Remember, while maintaining this single thought of who am I? the mind will return its attention to its original source, and the thought that arose will become dormant or quickly diminish.

Eventually, with continual practice in this manner, the mind will develop its ability to remain at its source without having the experience of being this-or-that even while experiencing the experience. This experience is the full actualization and realization of I am — meaning I exist as this-or-that. Even more organically, pure consciousness experiencing its enfoldment as consciousness in the formless state of I AM. This is the only true statement that can be made concerning its existence. You may be thinking to yourself, how is I AM to be experienced? There is no how-to- approach when it comes to experiencing the I AM, except just-be, without being this-or-that. This non-descriptive existence is a feeling of presence-awareness that extends beyond the intellect and any applications of how-to's.

The more you practice this feel sense of awareness, you will eventually create balance within your 'mind' and the 'feel' state causing both to merge as one; firmly establishing the thought-feeling of I AM." This sense of self remains as the ever-present backdrop within the mind that distinctively expresses its sense of presence through various forms of expressions— your thoughts, words, and actions. Even through the illusionary mental projections of being this-or-that. I have come to realize that I am neither this-or-that nor the mind or body — But the I AM in consciousness; a phenomenal presence that transcends the thinking mind and the five senses of the body.

If the enquiry of, who am I? was just sheer mental questioning, it would not be of much value. The extraordinarily purpose of self-enquiry is to focus the attention of the entire mind at its source to avoid the illusion of one 'I' in search for another 'I' to establish the I AM as being this-or-that. Which only create a dual existence between *self* and *other*. This concept of *self* and *other* falls into the realm of dualism, which warrants another conversation with a new line of questioning. As long as man possesses a curiosity and a desire to know his essence, the question will always exist and lead to more questions; an unending cycle that never produces a sufficient answer. Simply because you can only know yourself in desires, habits, likes, and dislikes.

However, there is a dynamic feature embedded within the question component of self-inquiry, an unknowable space that perpetuate its order of sequence in the forms of questions where questions cease to exist. So, for the curious mind this idea of the unknowable leads us to the question of its opposite, can that which is known come to know the knower? I leave you with this question to ponder for your own introspection. Self-inquiry is not an empty formula, for it involves intense activity involving the entire mind, giving its total and continuous attention to the awareness of self.

Self-enquiry is the one and only direct infallible means to realize the unconditioned being that you really are. Being able to identify and make the distinction between the observer and the observed that exist within you.

During this discovery, the mind often plays tricks by using the multiple I's of your personality to modify the perceived presence of both the observer and the observed within the one who claims to be observing. This is a false perception produced by the egoic mind that makes you believe that you are both. But, if you manage to focus your attention in the awareness of the I AM only, you will immediately eliminate the false projections of impressions within and the baffling thoughts of who is the observer and who is the observed. Both of which are an imaginary reflection of the abiding 'I' that is framed in the mirror of duality. So, once coming into the realization of this mental play the answer to the question should no longer rest in your mind.

Because the real answer arises from deep within the 'I' itself, and without it you would not be able to ask the question Who am I? So, when you pose the question Who am I? in hopes of pinpointing your true identity you will never find it, any more than an eye that can see its own seeing or seeing sees its own eye. An eye cannot see itself. However, in higher consciousness, you become devoid of any trace of objectivity that you cannot see, find, grasp, or attain. Because that which is sought is the seeker, and that which is looked-for is the looker. This is considered to be non-seeing yet while seeing by which you can differentiate between appearance and its source. But once the imaginary objects dissolve with its linking thoughts, you immediately realize that the asker of the question is the answer— both being one of the same. So then, the oscillation between the question-and-answer cease to be, gradually vanishing away as the day fades into the night and night into day; instead, it is an instantaneous apperception that extend beyond polarity, time, and space.

CHAPTER 5

REALIZING YOUR TRUE NATURE

————————— ●■● —————————

By now, you may have come to understand that you are neither your body nor your mind as it relates to the question of Who am I? Also, you may have realized that the true 'I' cannot be found via the intellectual mind. However, in your quest to know 'Who am I' requires a deeper plunge into the inquiry of self in order to find the answer to this insightful question. Remotely, the closes you will ever come to the answer is to have some degree of awareness of this existing 'I' without knowing the 'I' itself. For there is no knowable capacity within your mental faculty to know the unknowable. If you were to ask the average person Who or what he or she is? normally, they respond by using titles, labels, or something they do. Such as, I am a doctor, lawyer, human being, person, father, mother, etc.... you get my point. Your true self extends beyond classifications. All descriptions of any kind are creations of the conscious mind processed through intellectual analysis, logical deduction, and endless imaginings. The individual 'I' is independent in its subsistence to is bodily parts, and if the parts were removed, still, the real 'I' would remain.

The body is just a quantifiable assemblage of a physical abstract constructed in human form to house the I'ness of your being. In this realization, concepts cease to be, no goal to be reached, nothing to be attained or any expected outcome to be achieved. The I presence is forever present in the space of awareness, witnessing God as yourself, emanating an impulse of consciousness into manifested expression from the unmanifested Self. Such enfoldment becomes a eureka moment for the inquirer, meaning I have found. As a result of this direct experience, all falsely perceived notions that you are both mind and body instantly fall away.

Nonetheless, one must remain watchful of the crafty manipulation conducted by the ego because it can quickly assume the identity of any 'I' within the sub-personalities at will to deceptively assert its existence as being the real I– Self. Ultimately, the ego's tactic is designed to prevent you from turning inwardly toward the real 'I' in order to maintain its rule and reign. The ego will further reinforce its position by using your emotions and sensations aroused within the mind and body, so that you will continue to think you are both. This is only a distraction to cause you to abandon the question Who am I? and cease from your continuation of inquiry. This is the way the ego paints a portrait of reality and not reality itself. Just as the description is not the described, the map is not the territory nor is the menu the meal. The only way to counter this clever act of ego is to be persistent in your question of Who am I?

As you continue to inquire, you will realize that your innate awareness extends beyond your body and mind to include the five senses, however, going inward to inquire is the only effort necessary on your part. The mind is always occupied with thinking thoughts, creating ideas, or busy seeking some form of mental stimulations but never with your true self. If you desire to experience yourself in the most natural way, all you have to do is pause for a moment:

- ❖ Find a quiet location and sit comfortably with your back strait, chin slightly tucked with hands placed on both knees and feet spread twelve inches apart.
- ❖ close your eyes and relax your entire body by deeply inhaling and exhaling slowly through your nostril.
- ❖ Inhale and exhale for a one minute, in order to bring into focus your center of beingness.

❖ Be aware of your own existence and drop every thought about yourself to include your feelings, cares, concerns, personal identity, and all external attachments. Even the false definitions, expressions and tendencies associated with your personhood all of which you are not.

Unfortunately, the majority of people think of themselves as being the body and mind. In fact, this faulty thinking causes them to remain in the blitz of ignorance that bounds them to their carnal insatiable appetites. The only way to transcend this sort of thinking with its cravings, one must redirect his attention to the awareness of the true self during his self-enquiry. Which allows him to elevate in consciousness and commune with his higher Self. Failure to do so causes unwanted sufferings. But when you function from your higher self, you function from a noumenon state that is abstract in nature where there is no object to suffer. Because the noumenon is timeless, an unmanifested and non-phenomenal aspect of who we are as sentient beings.

On the other hand, there is the phenomenon aspect of our being that attends all manifestation that is subject to time, which allows us to experience pain and pleasure whereas the noumenal cannot experience either. Nonetheless, both play a role in the false sense of 'I', with the tendency to project their presence by using the words 'I am' which is most noticeable while engaged in conversation with others. More often than not, these two powerful words 'I am' are the first to emerge that presents a sense of beingness without understanding the misappropriation we lend to them. It is important to observe this expression quietly, and ask yourself from where does this announcement of 'I am' come from? Could it come from personalities within the personhood? describing itself as a personal noun not realizing the inherent power in these words. So, by using them in such casual ways to express our personal reference point, we compromise and minimize the authenticity of the true 'I AM'— the first born of the unmanifested 'I'.

However, as long as we stay focus on 'I AM' with a sustained amount of attention, we enter a state consciousness that goes beyond words that cannot be uttered or written but experienced only. After all, the sense of 'I AM' is always with you. Its existence is independent of any false identities you may have assigned or attached to it, such as your body, feelings, thoughts, or possessions, which are all derivatives of the personhood. He who yearns to know his true nature must first understand the false projections and mistaken identities displayed through perceptual objects such as I am this, or I am that. All identifications are temporary and consequently unreal. Associating the 'I' with 'this or that' takes one further from his authentic Self, because identifications lack permanency in all stages of life, except for the true 'I'. In this conclusion, the question 'Who am I?' will be found to have no answer, for what inherently exist? You cannot experience what is permanent in an objective or perceivable way, but only what you are not.

Your fundamental being cannot be reasoned or put into words that adequately describes your true existence because it is a non-dualistic state of 'be' that is constant, and omnipresent within humanity. In order to know who and what you are, you must first realize what you are not. This is conducted in an objective way through reasoning deductions through the process of elimination followed by self-analysis of your phenomenon state. This process normally causes one to transit inwardly toward his true source of being, eliminating all attachments and granting him the opportunity to become aware of himself as I AM— the Divine, rather than I am— this or that, which is not the fundamental truth of his true existence. Such as, I am my mind, I am my body, or I am my experience.

All of which are not the actual inherent 'I' in the sense of 'I am' even though the common belief among many are I am—this or that. In this moment, I want you to conduct a short experiment by eliminating the 'this or that' and persevere the 'I am' and feel what it means to be without the sense of being—this or that. Sit with this idea for a moment and ponder it is meaning to see what your awareness presents. In my experience, you will immediately feel a sense of emptiness, loneliness and none-existing— a place of nothingness. Which does not set well with the ego because it desperately needs the element of 'this or that' in order to thrive and feel alive. Without this element the ego cannot exist, and it will fight endlessly to keep its seemly threatened position to maintain its existences for past, present, and future validation. By perpetrating to be the real 'I' of the 'I am' disguising itself as being 'this or that'.

The sooner you understand the interplay between the ego and its coconspirators— sub-personalities, the quicker you will cease searching for an identity to be 'this or that'. And attune to your imperceptible 'I', the timeless and limitless noumenon Self, which is a 'no-thing'— non perceivable. Verses the phenomena of the temporal, finite, and perceptible 'I am' as being 'this or that'— descriptions that are created and imputed by ego. This or that is an imaginary description of 'self' that is impermanent and is an illusory figment in phenomena manifestation that is bound by time and space within a framework of a make-believe-world— dream state.

After all that has been said, can you be absolutely certain that you are neither the mind nor the body but pure consciousness? This is a question only you can answer, so any conclusion made must be by you alone. The core of your essence is the divine nature that serves as the substratum and underlay that give rise to every experience— be it thought, feeling, perception, sensation, or expression. The enfoldment of such discovery is disclosed within your awareness, which takes you beyond the idea of knowing anything about yourself. Because the 'knower' you do not know, just as the perceived cannot be the perceiver. Remember, you are not 'what happens' or 'who it happens-to', but rather the one to whom it 'happens-for' in whatever you see, hear, or think.

This is the law of grace in operation, and it is always working in your favor for the greater good even when you are not aware of it. But at the same time this infinite presence will aid in your pursuit of the pathless space of 'I AM'—the unmanifested existence of consciousness. When you think 'I AM' and only that, you liberate yourself from the bondage of identifications and emotional attachments. But the moment you consciously say: I am 'this or that' you risk falling into the falsehood of identifications with its sticky attachments. However, when you pose the question to yourself, who am I? you immediately return to the pure state of consciousness where the 'I' subsists; dissolving any traces of the personhood.

There are other states of consciousness to consider, the waking state, dream state, and deep sleep state, deriving from the timeless dimension of pure consciousness. These three states of consciousness generally trigger a relative sense of reality within the awareness of a person who is experiencing them. So, who is the one experiencing these various states? You are, and who are you? You are consciousness and what is consciousness? It is beyond description. The moment you answer the question or assign a description to it, you falsify its noumenal existence and make it into another object only to reflect half-truths. Consciousness, in the traditional meaning is Spirit, which cannot be known in the typical sense of the word, any attempt seeking to know it is futile. Because this type of knowing is ingrained in the realm of duality, being a subject and object, as is the knower and the known.

The 'I' is the knower of the 'I' only, without which nothing could be known, perceived, or felt but remains forever unknowable. This is because the 'I' has no form, it is only in form that things can be known or at lease known of. Yet without the formless dimension of the infinite space, the world form could not be. It is from this same timeless and eternal space that 'I Am' emerges and descend from the heavenly realms and spirals into the relative realms of duality. Which consist of pleasure and pain, gain and loss, and birth and death etc. The subline essence of 'I AM' is omnipresent, and how is it that we do not notice it? It is because your attention is set on external things. In the world of duality mental discrimination is necessary, in order to escape the erroneous thoughts of being 'this or that'. This bias approach allows you to regain your focus and redirect your attention to the internal aspect of your essence; without being mentally fixated on any particular thing.

In light of this process, you may be asking yourself, how does one transcend the realm of duality that contains both 'this and that'? the key is to mentally focus your attention on 'I AM' without adding 'this or that to it. This method quickly dissolves the dual existence of 'this or that' and the entire idea of separateness will no longer be your reality. Because you would have expanded in your awareness in spite of forms, perceptions, and appearances. Everything is interconnected within absolute consciousness; it is embedded in all that exist, even the element of life bares its imprint. Nothing in existence is separate as to subsist alone, but only appears to be in various forms just as you and I. But on a deeper level of consciousness, that adhesively binds us all, we are one— an extension of one another.

In so much my internal discovery of experience become your internal discovery of experience. Because the totality of life is experienced in the consciousness of 'IAM', and nothing else can ever exist beyond that except for pure consciousness and its emerging 'I'. Which makes you more conscious of being conscious by saying or thinking 'I Am' without adding to it. While at the same time being aware of the soundlessness, motionlessness and beingness that follows the 'I AM'. Sense its presence and allow it to usher you into the inner sanctum of its existence, which is the infinite womb that gives birth to all creation and its outward appearances. You may occasionally struggle with some of these concepts written in this book, but do not let it stop you from gravitating toward the 'I AM' presence within you.

The more you practice being aware of the 'I AM' essence, you will instantly ascend to a timeless space where there is no record of yesterdays or forecast of tomorrows. The 'I AM' exist with certainty but the 'I am, this-or-that' does not. Which brings us back to the question 'who am I?' From a perspective of higher consciousness, there is only one question, and the asker of this question is the answer. in other words, the question and the asker are one of the same. The question 'who am I?' only indicates that 'I' exist and is the only permanent self-evident and direct experience of my beingness, and there is nothing else as evident as 'I AM'. This state of consciousness requires no beliefs or assigned identities that may suggest that I am this-or-that.

Just be... be 'I AM' only, thus being imperceptible, infinite, an omnipresent— everywhere at all times, here and now in this present moment. When the focus remains stead-fast and stayed on 'I AM', Instantaneously and without notice, all your preconceived notions of who and what you are vanishes. Suddenly you realize, the influence of ego ceases to exist with its desire to be this-or-that, which normally causes unnecessary suffering. The 'I AM' is your inner compass that guides you along the uncharted course of its infinite station of 'BE' without the contamination of being this-or-that. There is nothing as effortless as being I AM.

CHAPTER 6

THE PERFECTION
OF A MASTER

●■●

When we humans achieve this fusion, our physical, mental, emotional, and spiritual behavior is then completely in accord with divine laws and fully reflects the greatness, beauty, and wisdom of Universal Intelligence.

To give you an idea of this Perfection, it is perhaps best to think about the example given by such individuals as Moses, 4 Rosicrucian Order AMORC Neophyte Section Atrium 3 Number 8 Buddha, Jesus, and Muhammad—to cite only the most well-known—for, after having received Illumination, their lives fully expressed the effects produced by the state of consciousness they had attained. They were no longer subject to any selfish desire and no longer experienced pride, jealousy, hypocrisy, or all those faults that constitute the weaknesses of ordinary human beings. They focused their entire being on goodness and used all their will to serve the God of their Heart. Given that they lived in perfect harmony with Cosmic Consciousness, they had at their disposal the powers necessary to carry out their mission. In this respect, the "miracles" attributed to them provide perfect testimony of this fact, as they prove that those individuals who have reached the state of Perfection, or are near it, become direct agents of the most sublime natural laws. Irrespective of the religions to which they gave birth, the way in which those Great Initiates lived can only arouse our admiration and give us the desire to elevate ourselves toward such a state of consciousness. It is relatively easy to imagine the virtuous life we will lead when we have attained Divine Perfection. On the other hand, it is much more difficult to understand how to proceed in order to achieve such Perfection in a single earthly life. When we take the time to consider the matter, how can we imagine that we may become perfect on all levels within only a few decades? From a purely logical point of view, such a thing is impossible. That is why the Rosicrucian Masters have always felt that human evolution can only be explained by resorting to the doctrine of reincarnation. However, we must emphasize at this time that you are entirely free to accept or reject this doctrine. We even need to point out that some members of our Order do not adhere to this doctrine, as it does not agree with their personal convictions. Yet that does not prevent them from being sincere Rosicrucians and from contributing fully to the expansion of spirituality. Nevertheless, reincarnation has always been part of our teachings. It is our duty, therefore, to transmit to you the knowledge of mystical laws relating to it.

Printed in the United States
by Baker & Taylor Publisher Services